AF449951

eRoseONE

rosepublish

gorithm

DGE RE

tificial i

g ·············
guage Pr
ssing Ta

tasks th
nual adv
hand c

deleted

irn from
s machir

rogramm
PUTD(
RIGHT

ɔ appear
ɑtural laɪ

re not v
 on your

n in Art

ificial I

f the pr

search c

e how s

hm exaı

:, graph

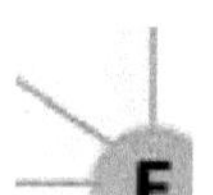

vertices

of the to

use of 1

Search A

ep using

y empty,

the sta

Glossaire

)(V * V)

ıtial com

tex c is r
place im

e data st

he best a
hile loo
test rout

ements.

orithm

will adva
ent state
vill beco

sing to i

the A*

he heuri

the fun

Weighted

not be a
ited the
irther in

ge, and a

tematic

ates the

ersonali
f all of l

, while
: has bee
based or

ıse ıs tn
ection o
ly. For i

ɔle to ac
verthele
ɔ-efficiei

evant so
equired 1

:ions for

ıg Prop

nclusion

rain), ha

true and
emands,

predicat
variable

ces.

, then L

mputer s
whether

n by ass
l predica

ve | Thi

of | Wit

(CNF)

nd assig

ence, {E
en able t

a comp
use of
that

lays do

colors,

nan, mot

rence ru
onclusio

› to bed"

y nome
key ther

n. ==> P
ream.

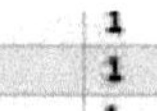

y | NM
ɔt | reas
| its d

$$= \frac{0.0}{0.}$$

he car m

ls the t
r instanc

or the ra

ities hav

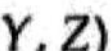
$Y, Z)$

'(cavity, to

equired

$$p(h \mid E)^{l}$$

a means

ut the r

$$= \frac{0.8 * (\frac{1}{3000}}{0.02}$$

tion is in

iations o

the prob
. To ac
\ or the

rom thir

:mantic

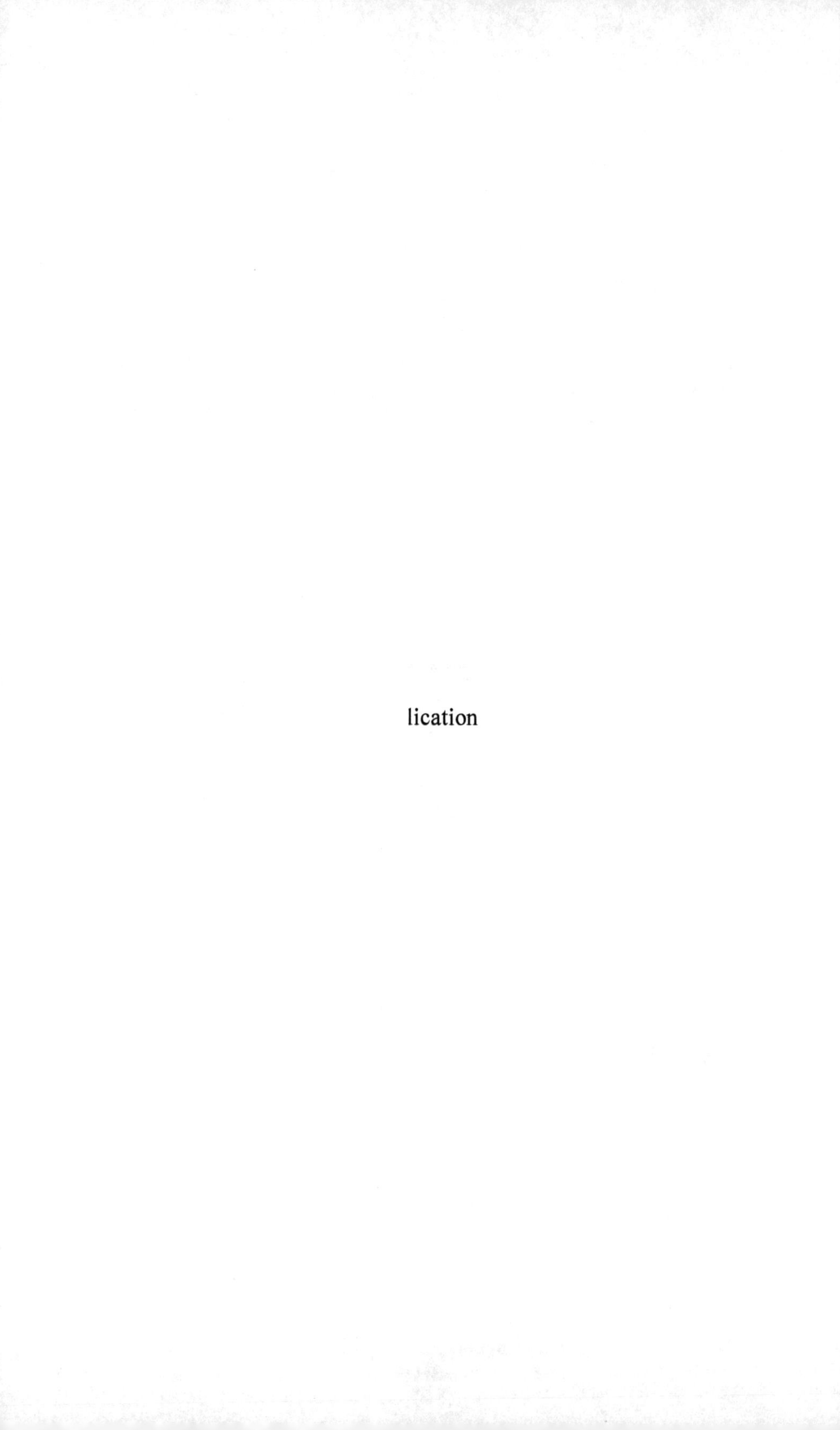

lication

fications

they ar

repre

etween

ce in ord

:sent all

formation

ightforw
monkey

0 Main St

phase,
d impler

t will m
·s, and

ssion by

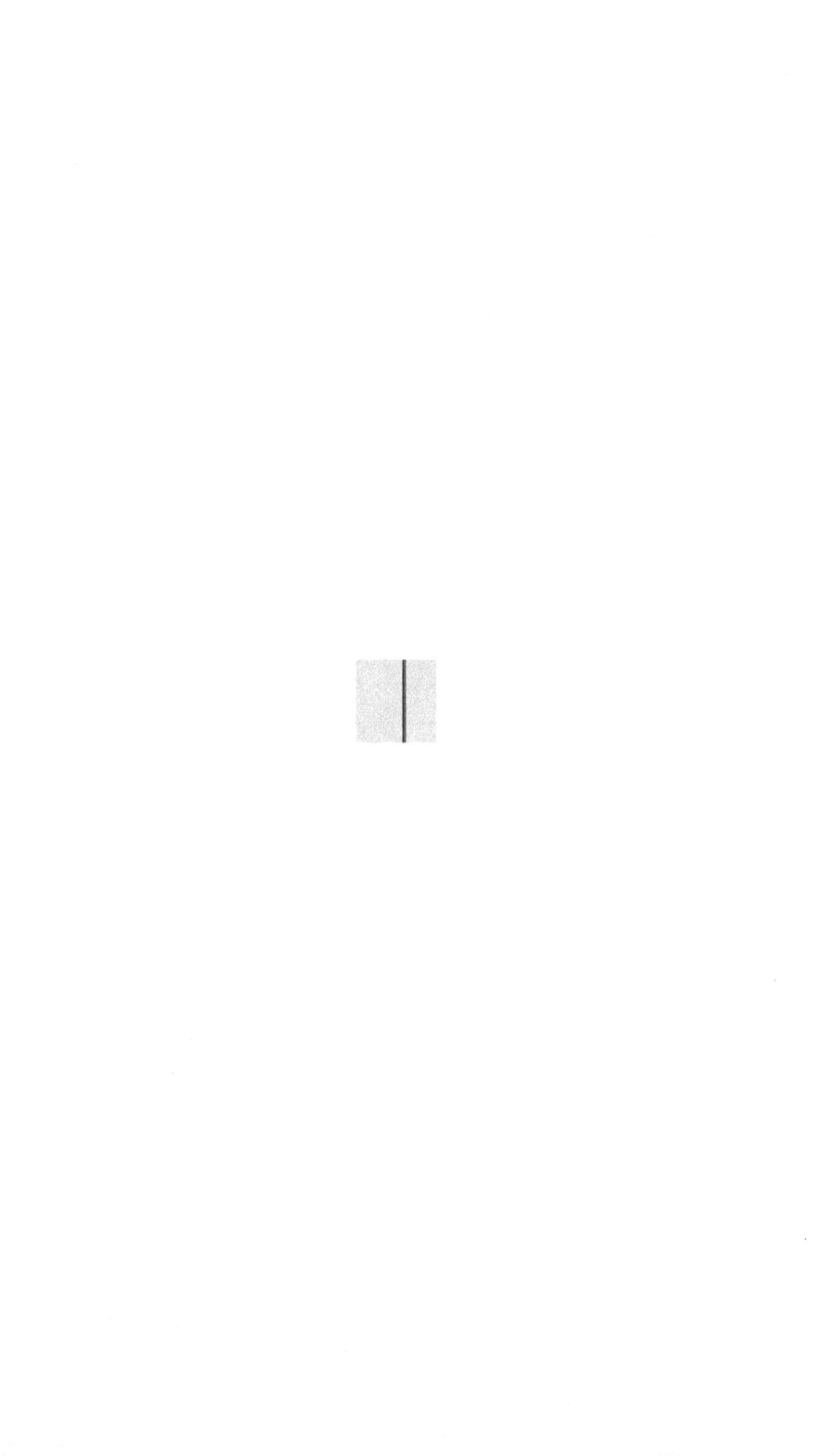

enefits (

11

Ten

nberships
ate the s

ss will b

forward

area of
that is re
of winni

conflict
ie impac

gives mit

-5   0

M
N
-5
0

s includ

further

nown a

en to 3,
de value

ade P

e 1 to no
ompared
a criteric

rd scena
onably p
llange w

:o reach

gorithm

tack to b

ick is a r

ning for

to be acc
:complis

c

D List 1

ecuted.

ists for

ıding en
ic analy

rom ele

d data. N

ing plat

istics, w

ord is be

two oth

·d's mea
1er as a
is in the

t freque
ıt are n

views, c
icts, pro
product

to genu
d to be a
· perspe

ummari

ocess o

ransforn

onable 1
velop bt

that sho
"What s

ons that
 for the
f the pr

ormance

those c

ormance
his man

ction sh
n in Fig

nfluence
r not the

or chara
id in the

ance, we

hould st
e refer to
test imp

ise in t
ient info
elf is ac

Feature
Some
X1,X3,X6

ungry?

ɔ catego
escribed

of real e
provide i

learning
in the d

of Ar

ssificatic
l insight
and bus

ıral lang
puter sy

ernal ser
hestratio

y artifici

ıple visı

e anoth

elligenc
dels, and
many c

e are re
rained N

n the sur
l is allov

;hted tot
an activ

vorks

work ar

cular pro
n sense i

alists ma
t their s
a season

Univer
of VCF

sion of p
on or fir

out ever

nformat

he additi

e: This
is found

N-ELSE

ɔm mista